AF455238

'Roycraft':
Western New York Craft and its Inclusion in Contemporary Crafts Curriculum

by

Megan L. Westenfield

First Printing, 2012

ISBN 978-1-105-74139-5

www.lulu.com

Roycraft:
Western New York Craft and its Inclusion in Contemporary Crafts Curriculum

by

Megan L. Westenfield

An Abstract of a Thesis
in
Art Education

Submitted in
partial fulfillment of the requirements for
the degree of Masters of Science in Art Education

Nazareth College of Rochester
Department of Art Education
Rochester, New York
May, 2012 (receiving M.S. degree)

ABSTRACT OF THESIS

'Roycraft':
Western New York Craft and its Inclusion in Contemporary Crafts Curriculum

The purpose of this research study is to determine whether or not local craft resources are being utilized as part of contemporary craft classes in Western New York. The area of Western New York is rich with craft resources, from the early twentieth century pioneers, to current contemporary craft artists. The literature states that craft education is beneficial to student learning, and influences students in a positive manner. The method of this study is qualitative in order to shed light on this issue. I utilized interviews as the primary data collection method, as well as curriculum reviews. Participants include most of the school districts in the Western New York region, including Buffalo, Niagara, Rochester and surrounding areas. In order to gain a better understanding of teaching, curriculum maps from three local school districts were obtained and analyzed. Other participants include three art teachers from the Western New York Region, as well as the program director for The Roycroft Campus Corporation. By analyzing the data it was determined that there is a disconnect between what art teachers feel is important, and what was actually taught in their classrooms. Art teachers understand the value of craft, yet expressed that they cannot find a way to successfully integrate local craft into their curriculum.This study's findings suggest that local craft resources such as the Roycroft are reaching out to educators, yet they are not successful due to a number of concerns. Concerns such as budget are a major issue for promoting the crafts in Western New York. More research may need to be done in order to fully understand the disconnect between art teachers and local Western New York Craft.

‘Roycraft’:
Western New York Craft and its Inclusion in Contemporary Crafts Curriculum

by

Megan L. Westenfield

B.S. in Jewery Design, Buffalo State College, 2009

Presented in
partial fulfillment of the requirements for
the degree of Masters of Science in Art Education

Nazareth College of Rochester
Rochester, New York
May, 2012 (receiving M.S. degree)

This thesis is dedicated to Stephen R. Saboda, who always finds a way to make my passions his passions.

And also to my parents, Tony and Christine Westenfield,who have taught me the value of working with my hands.

TABLE OF CONTENTS

INTRODUCTION 1

REVIEW OF THE LITERATURE 5

METHODOLOGY 18

DISCUSSION 22

ANALYSIS 31

CONCLUSION 33

REFERENCES 36

APPENDICES 39

Introduction

It is only by labor that thought can be made healthy, and only by thought that labor can be made happy, and the two cannot be separated with impunity. It would be well if all of us were good handcraftmen in some kind, and the dishonor of manual labor done away with altogether.

- John Ruskin, 1853

For much of my formative years craft has been an influence in my life, and I was not even aware of it. My father is a Union carpenter and woodworker, and my mother is a talented seamstress. They both can relate to the statement above by John Ruskin, about the importance of craft. I grew up in an environment where it was more appropriate to make something than to purchase it. As a young person I believed most households must be like mine, yet as I grew older I found that this is not true. This background has shaped my own philosophy, and my perception of art and craft. Through my education and personal exploration I have come to fully embrace craft, and the philosophy of the Arts and Crafts movement. I believe that other students should be given the opportunity to learn and understand craft, and be influenced by it.

The Western New York area, of which I grew up in, is rich with craft resources. The area from Buffalo to Syracuse is well known among art historians as the incubator for the Arts and Crafts movement in the United States (Ludwig, 1983). Arts and Crafts historian Robert Rust (2012) teaches about the importance of this region in art history to such far away places as Australia (personal communication, February 17, 2012). Art and design historians understand the importance of Western New York, yet do the residents and students of this region understand its historical and cultural importance? This research study hopes to shed light on the question of how is the history and culture of craft in Western New York reflected in the contemporary crafts curriculum of selected Western New York districts?

In my own Kindergarten through grade 12 art experience I was not made aware of the Arts and Crafts movement, and our proximity to many historic sites. I grew up thirty minutes from where the Roycrofters founded their utopian, craft society, yet I did not know this until I was in my undergraduate studies at Buffalo State College. I have found that this experience is not unique; that many others are not aware of local craft resources until college, or not at all. As I progressed through education and became a jewelry and metals design major, through classes and research I finally found the wealth of craft resources in my own backyard.

Through education and past experiences, my personal definition of craft may differ from others. Many researchers, theorists, and educators cannot agree on a definition of craft, which in my opinion adds to craft's status issue. For the purpose of this study, the definition of craft must be explored and defined. I have also included my personal definition of craft which has influenced my research, and may have biased opinions and analysis of research.

Craft is often situated outside the realm of fine art. Its status is vague, and even the word 'craft' is debated within the craft community itself (Dormer, 1997). But, what exactly is craft? Craft can encompass a wide variety of visual artifacts, and its status is constantly changing (Metcalf, 2010). Craft is presented by Greenhalgh (2002), the head of research at the Victoria and Albert Museum, as, "...a fluid set of practices, propositions and positions that shift and develop rapidly"(p. 1). Although, The Crafts Council (2005), an international group of craft advocates, has defined craft as, "the act of making, manipulating and sensory experience of materials, the acquisition of practical forms of knowledge that are tactile, intuitive and skills-based and involve aesthetic qualities such as craftsperson-ship." This definition is convoluted, and does not do craft justice. A clearer and concise definition of craft would help the understanding of craft, and possibly raise its status within the art community.

For this reason, a more accurate definition of craft is closer to that of Mason's (2005), which associates the word 'craft' with four constructs and processes. These constructs and processes are neglected in current art and design theories. Mason defines craft as, "Namely (i) the act or activity of making; (ii) skilled knowledge; (iii) craftspersonship, which plays a hugely significant role in aesthetic judgement and (iv) apprenticeship - a form of learning that is intuitive and which knowledge and skills are acquired through modeling and practice" (Mason, 2005, p. 262). Mason's language mimics some of the same rhetoric as The Crafts Council, yet her definition is clearer. Mason argues that craft is something that a skilled person creates with careful recognition of aesthetics, and shows the influence of many years of training.

Currently the field of craft is migrating in many directions. The influence of websites such as Etsy and Pinterest give craft artists a marketplace and audience for craft products. Although this brings access and business to many craft artisans, it also allows for any nature of items to be labeled craft. I do not agree with some of the products that are currently labeled craft. Therefore for the purpose of this study, craft is not old furniture that is painted and repurposed as wood craft, nor is it a machine-made coffee mug with a mustache painted on it. My sentiments are echoed by the writer and blogger April Winchell (2010), creator of Regretsy.com and author of *Regretsy: Where DIY meets WTF.* Winchell brings attention to the more unfortunate and humorous expressions of "craft" that some contemporary artists are presenting. She adds to the discussion of what is and is not craft with her own wit and humor.

From research and personal knowledge, a more realistic definition of craft is a combination of many listed previously, and is more traditional than contemporary. I feel that craft is a process which creates objects that are often functional or wearable. These objects are handmade by someone who has spent time perfecting their skills. There is a level of knowledge and mastery associated with craft, and each craft object should show the mark of the craftsman. Marking each crafted piece offers an emotional significance for the craftsman and consumer that cannot be obtained by a mass-produced, machine created product. This emotional significance of craft has influenced my research and perception, and it has also lead me to be passionate about craft in the Western New York area.

I have been influenced by research on the importance of the Arts and Crafts movement in the United States. Some of this research study has focused on the Western New York Region. Historians and authors Rust and Turgeon (1999) have explored this topic in depth. Although there is much research and writing dedicated to the history of the Arts and Crafts Movement in Western New York, there is none that focuses on craft in visual arts curriculum in this region.

Because of the lack of research regarding the specific topic, I have pulled resources from many areas. I will explore craft history of the 19th and 20th centuries, craft in education, and the importance of craft in the Western New York area, in an effort to show a more rounded picture of craft, and how it could be influential to students. By viewing contemporary crafts curriculum, and interviewing teachers and historians I hope to find whether or not the history and culture of craft is being presented to K through 12 art students in Western New York.

Literature Review

Craft has been identified in the past as the decorative arts (Dormer, 1997). The term craft has been used to identify objects like furniture, glass, ceramics, metalwork, tapestry, and jewelry only more recently in art history. Greenhalgh (1997) argues that the decorative arts are a disenfranchised art, and have never been recognized in the same category as the Fine Arts. The division of craft is an essential aspect to understanding craft's history. Because of craft's disenfranchised status by many in art history, craft is not seen to be as important as the Fine Arts (Greenhalgh, 1997). The research contends that the status of craft has lead to its current location of less prominence underneath Fine Art in galleries and in art education curriculum.

Although craft's status is less than ideal, the history of craft is vast and colorful, like craft artifacts themselves. Because craft history is so vast, for the purpose of this study a highly condensed exploration of the literature is presented. Humans have been making craft items for all of history, yet, one can argue that the craft movement of the late 19th and 20th century seems to serves as a foundation for our modern interpretation of craft and its position in the art world. By analyzing history, a primary catalyst can be found for the Arts and Crafts movement of the late 19th and 20th centuries is the industrialization and modernization of European culture (Dormer, 1997). Anti-modernists wanted to find a way to preserve tradition, and many activists and writers wanted to voice their unhappiness with this new focus on machines and factories.

Greenhalgh (2002) researched the English writer John Ruskin, who was one of these activist writers. Ruskin was born in 1819, to a family that fully supported art and knowledge (Boris, 1986). Ruskin graduated from Oxford and soon his name became synonymous for literature critiquing art and architecture of the period. Historian and researcher Boris (1986) felt that Ruskin gained support of many through his demand of functional materials, and honest structure. He also called for recognizing the mark of the craftsman, which was contrary to the industrialized products coming out of European factories. Greenhalgh explains Ruskin's contempt for industrialization, and how he believes that it dehumanizes man (2002). Ruskin's opinion is one that was beginning to be felt in many newly industrialized nations, as increasingly products were being created with the help of machines.

Coinciding with Ruskin and the anti-modernists, is the writing, art, and political views of William Morris. Morris is considered to be one of the most influential voice in the Arts and Crafts movement. Morris was a celebrated English textile artist, and created the decorative arts firm, Morris, Marshall, Faulkner and company (Boris, 1986). Morris had been known to plead for, " A world in which there was an enjoyment in labor through the regeneration of handcraft" (Greenhalgh, 2002, p. 38). The author Clancy (2009) describes Morris as "the acknowledged leader of the crafts revival who sought to soothe the anxieties of the modern period through medievalizing enterprise" (p. 149). Morris seems to have taken the lead of the Arts and Crafts movement, which has lead him to be a prominent figure of that period. However, one issue with Morris was his ardent embrace of socialism. Morris' Arts and Crafts movement ideal of the importance of the worker, reflected this embrace of socialism (Boris, 1986). Morris felt that the worker must be the focus of society, and this should be reflected in government. This was a more radical idea at the time, and many did not appreciate, or understand his sentiments. A detriment of this is Morris' political views often lead to more emphasis being placed on his socialist thoughts, and less on the craft he supported.

The influence of Morris migrated to the United States, where it manifested in various artworks. In the U.S., the burgeoning Arts and Crafts movement was evidenced with Charles Rohlfs and Gustav Stickley, both furniture makers (Cunningham, 2008). It was also seen in the glass work of Louis Comfort Tiffany (Kangas, 2006). Tiffany's lamps and jewelry were extremely popular and helped bring attention to the movement. Also integral to the advance of the Arts and Crafts movement in America was The Women's Pottery club of Cincinnati (Smith and Lucie-Smith, 1986). This club then became Rookwood pottery which was influential in developing pottery with innovative techniques and glazes. Other women's groups such as the Chicago Society of Decorative Art also added to the recognition of the Arts and Crafts movement. These groups had exhibitions at the World's Columbian Exhibition, also known as the Chicago world's fair, which in turn promoted the movement further (Smith and Lucie-Smith, 1986).

As the influence of craft became more apparent, small Arts and Crafts communities began forming in the United States. Communities and havens such as Marblehead in Massachusetts, and Arequipa Sanitarium in Fairfax, California recognized the importance of the crafts (Ludwig, 1983). Within this state the Oneida community in Oneida, New York, and the Byrdcliffe colony in Woodstock, New York were both important in promoting the movement (Ludwig, 1983). Institutions like the Chautauqua Institute were integral in promoting the Arts and Crafts philosophy, even if there primary concern was not with the creation of craft items (Ludwig, 1983). From the research, one of the most notable of these communities was The Roycroft of East Aurora, New York (Rust & Turgeon, 1999).

The Roycroft was started as a printing shop in 1896 by Elbert Hubbard (Koch, 1967). Hubbard was a former executive who had started his own periodical named The Philistine, with writings based on the Transcendentalist writers, and anti-modernists like Ruskin and Morris. The writer Koch describes how scholars and craftsmen flocked to the small community outside of Buffalo, NY to be part of Hubbard's utopian, craft-oriented society. Here Roycroft artists became well known for their furniture, metalwork, textiles and printing (Koch, 1967).

After World War II, craft experienced a surge of popularity. Authors Smith and Lucie-Smith (1986) contend that an influx of able-bodied men after the war, who wanted to do honest work with their hands, led to an interest in woodworking, metalwork and ceramics. Universities and colleges began creating majors and courses in the crafts. One noted outcome of this was when Peter Voulkos went to teach at the Otis Art Institute in Los Angeles in 1954 (Smith, & Lucie-Smith, 1986). Voulkos was a well known potter at the time who took his work and pushed it away from the boundaries of craft, and closer to fine art. He was influenced by abstract expressionism, which was the major Fine Art movement at the time. Voulkos influenced other fine artists and craftspeople and led the way in blurring the line between art and craft (Smith, & Lucie-Smith, 1986).

Like Voulkos at the Otis Art Institute, the middle of the 20th century continued to be an era where American craft schools had a great affect and influence on craft artists (Kirwin and Lord, 2003). From the research, these schools include Haystack Mountain School of Craft in Deer Isle, Maine; Penland School of Crafts in Penland, North Carolina; Pilchuck Glass School in Stanwood, Washington; Arrowmont School of Arts and Crafts in Gatlinburg, Tennessee; and Anderson Ranch in Snowmass Village, Colorado. Authors Kirwin and Lord (2003) describe these craft schools as artistic communities where craftspeople of all mediums lived and worked together in a harmonious setting. The authors explain that these craft school settings and their 24 hour studios encouraged collaboration, and allowed craftspeople to learn from each other. These collaborations helped change craft, and allow it to evolve organically through the artists themselves.

As discovered in the research, craft has gone through many manifestations, to arrive at its present state (Dormer, 1997, Greenhalgh, 1997, Smith and Lucie-Smith, 1986). The well known metalsmith Bruce Metcalf (2010) believes that many of the same issues that early craft pioneers dealt with are still concerns today. According to Metcalf, these concerns include the hybridization of different materials, which is creating art works with many different materials. Other concerns are the embrace of the marketplace and consumerism, the inclusion of irony and kitsch to craft, and finally community activism. Metcalf also contends that many of the boundaries that have been historically separating art and craft are being broken down by young artists who feel that these boundaries are no longer valid, and that they limit their ability to make interesting and conceptual work. A conclusion might be drawn that as these boundaries remain blurry, and are constantly being pushed, it makes craft's place in the art world even more vague.

In addition to craft's unclear position within art history, craft's position within education may be just as dubious. Olafsson and Thorsteinsson (2009), researchers from the University of Iceland, fully examined craft education's history from the middle ages to present. They explained that within the Middle Ages, educationalists explored the importance of manual training as a way to establish a balance between the physical and mental faculties, and to prepare individuals for a better life. As Olafsson and Thorsteinsson's article progresses through history, they shed light on the principles of 17th century Comenius who stated, "...the fundamental principles of handicraft education and the importance of real life experiences. In order to learn, work should be done and the master should allow the disciples to learn through their own efforts, not just by him demonstrating the work to them" (Olafsson, & Thorsteinsson, 2009, p. 11). The essence of Comenius' argument therefore on the benefit of learning through real life experience could apply directly to modern education, even though the statement is over 350 years old.

Olafsson and Thorsteinsson (2009) examined the writings of Jean-Jacques Rousseau; the philosopher who lived from 1712 to 1778. According to Olafsson and Thorsteinsson, Rousseau wrote about education through his main character Emile. Rousseau believed people practicing craft were some of the happiest human beings on the earth, and because of that he wanted his main character, Emile, to learn woodcraft. His connecting characters to craft demonstrated a prominent philosopher's comprehension of the value of craft, and craft education.

In addition to highlighting historical advocates of craft education, Olafsson and Thorsteinsson (2009) addressed more recent craft advocates when describing the Sloyd pedagogy, which is a type of education prominent in Finland, Iceland, Sweden and Denmark. The Sloyd education refers to a program of, "...school activities which use craft to produce useful and decorative objects" (Olafsson, & Thorsteinsson, p.13).

Since Finland is one of the Nordic countries whose position on craft is favorable, they are seen as supportive of craft within their school system. Currently, in the Nordic countries mentioned previously, craft is a compulsory subject for all students in the National Core Curriculum for Basic Education (Pollanen, 2009). Researcher Pollanen (2009) contends that students identify with craft in many ways, which includes: craft as product-making, craft as skill and knowledge building, craft as design and problem solving, as well as craft as self expression. These are all areas of knowledge that seem to be beneficial to any student, not just students involved in the arts. This type of learning elludes to the involvement of a more student-centered approach, rather than a teacher dictating the aims of the lesson. Finland therefore is a particularly relevant example because of their success in the area of education.

In a document from the U.S. Department of Education entitled, Highlights From PISA 2009: Performance of U.S. 15-Year-Old Students in Reading, Mathematics, and Science Literacy in an International Context, which lists national testing scores in reading, math and science. Out of 65 participating countries, Finland can be found within the top five of every category. Success of this magnitude demonstrates an educational culture that excels in knowledge building and problem solving, two areas of learning that craft supports.

In contrast to the Nordic approach, craft education does not have as favorable of a status in other countries (Mason, 2005). For example, according to research, craft has disappeared from the National Curriculum in England altogether (Mason, 2005). In the United States craft classes and even art classes are not compulsory at the secondary level (Dormer, 1997). The artisan Bruce Metcalf (1997), who is also a professor of metalsmithing, found that most American student's first experience with craft was at the college level. He also explained that many of these students would not have any contact with craft again.

However, many educational researchers believe that craft can have a positive impact on student learning throughout their educational careers (Mason, 2005). Within the research of Metcalf, (1997) he expressed the definition of craft as explained by education philosopher Howard Gardner. Gardner defined craft as, "A distinctive form of skilled knowledge that is intuitive and expressed through making and doing." Gardner also believed that craft relates most closely to the bodily kinesthetic intelligence out of his seven intelligences (Mason, 2005). Metcalf (1997) stated that craft is a way for people to exercise their bodily kinesthetic intelligence; something that Western society provides few outlets for. I believe from the research that herein lies the problem. The bodily kinesthetic intelligence is often perceived to be lower on a hierarchical scale of intelligences when compared to mathematical or verbal. Yet, Gardner believes that there should not be a hierarchical order to these intelligences, and that all are equally important (Metcalf, 1997). It can be concluded that the hierarchical system of intelligences within a school system is contrary to what research presents, which could lead to disparity and discrimination among students, and possibly art teachers themselves.

Based on research, the bodily kinesthetic intelligence should be an integral part of any education system. As Metcalf (1997) stated, there are not many ways to exercise this particular intelligence in a western educational system. If more students were able to participate in crafts classes, where their bodily kinesthetic intelligence was exercised, they could produce something with their own two hands that they could be proud of. An outcome of this could be the promotion of self efficacy among students in the school environment.

With this in mind, it is important to note that to many the main goal of craft education is not to produce future craftsmen or artists. A researcher from the University of Helsinki, Seija Karppinen (2008), insists that, "...the purpose is to enable individuals' thinking into artistic thinking also in other situations. In other words, the purpose is to enable transformation in one's mind so that the new ways of thinking will also be evident in individuals' behavior, thoughts and products" (p. 87). To coincide with this, Karppinen also stated in his research that by practicing the crafts, and learning hand skills at an early age, these activities may help to produce future dentists or surgeons. According to Karppinen and his research, craft improves both mental and physical capabilities. It improves problem solving and creative thinking, while also improving hand-eye coordination and dexterity; all of which are useful skills in any career path (Karppinen, 2008).

Having outlined the importance of craft, in relation to history, education and the student, it is now important to revisit an area of related craft history. The region of Western New York, including Buffalo, Rochester and the surrounding areas, is highly influenced by the craft culture. Residents of this region have a unique opportunity to explore and learn from the crafts, and use our local resources to their fullest extent.

Some of the first influential craftsmen of the Arts and Crafts movement were furniture makers from the Western New York region. Charles Rohlfs worked in Buffalo, New York and Gustav Stickley worked in Syracuse, New York (Cunningham, 2008). Cunningham (2008) suggested that Rohlf's furniture designs predate Stickley's, but both men drew influence from each other, and were very competitive. When viewing the work of both men Rohlf 's work has a more ornate, art nouveau style, while Stickley's is more streamlined. Both men also showed their work at the Pan-American Exposition in Buffalo, NY in 1901, which helped to promote the Arts and Crafts movement to new observers. Rohlf's Arts and Crafts style home can still be found within the Allentown district of Buffalo, NY (Ludwig, 1983). This local landmark can serve as a constant reminder to locals about the area's illustrious Arts and Crafts history.

Stickley however became the more prominent of the two men, because of his legacy with the Craftsman workshops in Syracuse, New York. His furniture was made for use, comfortability, durability and beauty (Ludwig, 1983). This design aesthetic made him popular with many, and his designs are still influential today. Another way Stickley influenced the Arts and Crafts movement was through his magazine, *The Craftsman* (Ludwig, 1983). *The Craftsman* included a wide range of topics that were of interest to any Arts and Crafts supporter. Stickley also used his magazine as a way to improve public taste, and share his aesthetic with a broader range of individuals (Ludwig, 1983).

The influence and popularity of *The Craftsman,* other periodicals, and craft's communities seems to allow for schools and societies to be created with a focus on craft. In New York State alone The Rochester Arts and Crafts Society, The Mechanics Institute in Rochester, The New York State School of Clayworking and Ceramics at Alfred University, and The Pratt Institute in Brooklyn all had an early and profound affect on the Arts and Crafts movement in New York State (Ludwig, 1983). These schools taught, promoted, sold and refined craft in the early 1900s, by creating havens of learning and exploration. Some of these programs including Alfred University and the Pratt Institute still exist today.

Following next in history are the Roycrofters. These individuals who make up the Roycroft community, such as scholars, artists, workers and farmers, founded their home in East Aurora, NY. They created a community with workshops, a printing press, and even an inn for visiting artists and curious onlookers (Koch, 1967). The founder Elbert Hubbard believed, like Ruskin and Morris, that work should have meaning. Ludwig (1983) states that people should not shy away from labor, because through labor and creation one can find happiness. The essence of the Roycroft philosophy is the connection between the head, hand, and heart. Ludwig (1983) quoted Hubbard in defining the Roycroft spirit as, "A belief in working with the Head, Hand and

Heart, and mixing enough play with the Work so that every task is pleasurable and makes for Health and Happiness (p.36).

Koch (1967) argues that one artist whose work helped to shape and develop the Roycroft style was Dard Hunter. Many of designs of Elbert Hubbard's book covers were designed by Hunter. According to Koch, Hunter created 2-dimensional and 3-dimensional work that showed less influence of art nouveau, and more influence of the Viennese decorative art. This means that Hunter's work was more formal and simplified, with more emphasis on the rectangle and square. It has been noted by many art historians that Hunter's style was a great influence on the world renowned architect Frank Lloyd Wright (Rust & Turgeon, 1999). As explained by a docent at the Roycroft community, Frank Lloyd Wright even stayed at the Roycroft Inn with Elbert Hubbard when visiting the community (personal communication, March 11, 2012).

Another influential artist from the Roycroft was the metalsmith Karl Kipp (Turgeon, and Rust, 1997). Kipp expanded the Roycroft Copper Shop and created works that were truly unique in design and craftsmanship (Ludwig, 1983). Ludwig also felt that Kipp's association with Dard Hunter, and Hunter's influence of Viennese decorative art, gave both men their unique style of straight clean lines with the emphasis on squares and rectangles. Kipp eventually left the Roycroft to open his own metal's workshop, called the Tookay Shop, in East Aurora (Ludwig, 1983).

The Roycroft seems to be a continued source of inspiration and learning within the international craft community. Having visited the grounds of the Roycroft community, I have found many of the buildings restored, and new craft artists are teaching, working and learning in a similar community style as in the past. The teachers, historians, and docents of the Roycroft provide a great resource for learning about all aspects of this important movement and historic site. The Roycroft Inn, the Roycroft campus buildings, and even local homes such as the Alex Fournier home are a great resource to walk around and view beautiful, art, architecture, and craft from these master craftsmen of the early 20th century.

Another important player in the New York State Art and Crafts movement was Adelaide Alsop Robineau. This early 20th century artisan became a national force in promoting ceramics within the Arts and Crafts movement. She and her husband, Samuel Robineau, lived in Syracuse, New York and created the periodical *Keramic Studio* (Ludwig, 1983). The periodical started off with information geared towards amateur china painters, but soon became more technical and geared towards ceramic artists (Ludwig, 1983). The distribution of this periodical helped to inform other artists, and introduce new artists to ceramics.

Within the same region, another important landmark for craft can be found at the School for American Craftsmen at the Rochester Institute of Technology (RIT). Authors Koplos and Metcalf (2010) described the history of this school as first starting at Dartmouth College in 1944, then moving to Alfred University in 1946, before relocating to its present location at RIT. The initial emphasis at this school was the traditional craft areas such as furniture making, silversmithing and ceramics, yet in recent years this craft school has taken on other mediums and more modern progressions (Koplos & Metcalf, 2010). The website for the School for American Craftsmen states that it has undergraduate and graduate majors in metalworking, ceramics, glass and woodworking (http://cias.rit.edu/schools/american-crafts, 2012).

Next, within the same proximity of the School for American Craftsmen is an internationally known jewelry and metal artist whose studio is in Rochester, New York. Albert

Paley is known for his large scale metal sculptures that have graced the landscapes of countries all over the globe (Fariello, 2005). Paley began his career as a goldsmith, and then started creating in the craft of blacksmithing. The writer Anna Fariello describes the studio of Paley as a 20,000 square-foot studio, which employs eight people, and within the past 30 years has created over 50 large, site-specific pieces of metalwork. People can see Paley's work Sentinel (2003) on the grounds of the Rochester Institute of Technology, where Paley holds a professorship.

Continuing with the craft resources in the Rochester area is the furniture craftsman Wendell Castle. Castle and his wife, prominent ceramic artist Nancy Jurs, have lived in Monroe County since 1978 (Simpson, 1994). Castle has taught at the Rochester Institute of Technology, SUNY College at Brockport, and even operated the Wendell Castle school in Scottsville, New York from 1980 through 1988 (American Craft Council Awards, 1997). Koplos and Metcalf (2010) explain Castle as an experimental and freewheeling artist, as well as a teacher who created fertile environments for students to be creative. When viewing Castle's wood furniture designs, one notices his modern, clean approach, and a slight resemblance to the art of Pablo Picasso. From the Memorial Art Gallery of Rochester's website more of Castle's work can be seen as be part of their Phase 1 Centennial Sculpture Park to be completed in the near future (http://mag.rochester.edu/centennial-sculpture-park/phase-1/, 2012).

The Burchfield Penney Art Museum in Buffalo, NY has collections of all the artists mentioned from this region, along with many others that are not as well known. This museum is an excellent resource to explore the world of craft, and to learn about the culture and history of craft around us. Exploring the collection of The Burchfield shows viewers the work of early Arts and Crafts Movement artisans, as well as more modern craft artists. The Burchfield Penney is affiliated with Buffalo State College, which also has a well know craft design program. Buffalo State College has celebrated contemporary craft artists such as Robert Wood and Stephen Saracino as faculty members in their program. Buffalo State College happens to be my alma mater, and where my interest in local craft resources was first sparked.

Theoretical Frame

I analyzed my results accounting for the theoretical frame of postmodernism. This was pertinent to my study because of the relationship between the Fine Arts and craft throughout history, and within the local culture and art curriculum. Authors Zeeman, Poggenpoel, Myburgh, and Linde (2002) described postmodern theory as dismantling the normal way people view and think about reality. They also described it as, "The existence of more than one interpretation of the world and the thought that the self has more than one view..." (p. 96). This theory of postmodernism relates to the world of craft because craft is often viewed at a lower status than that of the Fine Arts, and I hope to challenge this long held interpretation with the implications of this study.

Methods

In order to pursue this research on how the history and culture of craft in Western New York is reflected in the contemporary crafts curriculum of selected Western New York districts I needed to use a variety of methodologies. Foremost, this was a qualitative study. Author David M. Fetterman (1988) believes that qualitative research is becoming more prevalent in educational studies. I chose qualitative research because I viewed the research through the theoretical frame of postmodernism, which allowed me to question long standing belief systems. My research has been conducted in a qualitative rather than quantitative manner because it is more about raising awareness on the idea of craft in Western New York, rather than to provide statistical data from which to draw conclusions.

To begin this study I collected data concerning which public school districts in Western New York offered craft courses as part of their visual arts curriculum. The school district area I researched was the Western New York region, which consists of the cities and surrounding communities of Rochester, Buffalo and Niagara Falls. The information was collected by researching school websites, and calling high school guidance counselors. Although this particular research is more quantitative in its data collection, it was essential for beginning my study.

Within this qualitative research study, I have reviewed the written school curricula of some Western New York contemporary crafts classes. The importance of both written curriculum and the more covert, internal curriculum within research is supported by authors Burnaford, Fischer, and Hobson (2001). These authors felt that teacher's curriculum was often shaped by their research. Although curriculum research is important, throughout education research history it was difficult to review curriculum due to the fact there is no one documented way to do it (Short, 1987). Edmund C. Short (1987) states that when reviewing and studying curriculum we have many methods, including ethnography, criticism, phenomenology, critical theory, and others, "But no authoritative handbook has yet appeared covering the variety of such approaches to curriculum inquiry" (p. 39). Due to this fact, I have chosen to review curriculum based on the qualitative research method of comparative inquiry.

In an article by Cummings (1999), the importance of comparing aspects of education was found to be essential to education research. Cummings believed that comparative inquiry was a part of the social sciences since its inception, and should continue to be a method for research. Cummings suggested that this type of research is important for highlighting similarities and differences throughout education. Because the society we live in is vast and diverse, I feel that one way to make meaning and understanding of issues is to compare them to each other.

Another methodology that was essential to my study was the interview. By interviewing participants, I obtained more detailed information on my subject matter. The qualitative interview has been described as one of the most important data gathering techniques in qualitative research (Myers & Newman, 2006). The type of interview conducted was described as a structured interview because of the fact that most of my interviews were conducted through asking a series of questions through email. Participants were asked to respond in a written format. A structured interview is described by Myers, and Newman (2006) as one where the script is already written out, and there is little room for improvisation. The participants in the study were all asked the same questions, a sample of which can be found in Appendix A. I also conducted more informal, unstructured interviews that can be described by Myers and Newman (2006) as having questions prepared beforehand, but also allowing for more improvisation, and more freedom for the researcher and interviewee to explore questions more thoroughly.

Participants

The participants in this study included most of the public school districts in the Western New York region. I researched course offerings of the schools in this area to determine whether districts had or did not have a Contemporary Craft or Studio in Craft course as part of their visual art department. Upon doing this, I decided to focus more closely at four specific school districts. This was a convenient sample based on access to information (Marshall, 1996). Three of these districts were suburban, public, school districts of mainly middle socioeconomic class. An additional suburban public school district of a lower socioeconomic class, which did not offer craft classes, was included for a more well-rounded perspective of craft in local schools

Other participants in this study included two teachers from the suburban, public, school districts of mainly middle socioeconomic class, which for the purpose of this study will be referred to as Teacher A and Teacher B. A teacher from the public school district of a lower socioeconomic class, which did not offer craft classes was also studied, and referred as Teacher C. The teachers I interviewed wished to remain anonymous. This is a convenient purposeful sample, based on the fact that these schools offered craft courses, were local, and they were able to be contacted for their curriculum information (Marshall, 1996). I have also obtained information advancing this study from a noted craft historian, and the Roycroft Campus Corporation Program Director. I have interviewed all of these participants as part of this research study. This study was an ongoing research process involving these various participants over a 12-week period.

Limitations

Since this research was done over a 12-week period as part of a capstone graduate class at Nazareth College, the major limitation of this study has been time. The scale of my research, and the number of participants was greatly reduced due to time constraints. In addition, the selection of schools and participants was based on access and availability. The sample size I have chosen is small, to be viable for the amount of time I had. This variable may account for some bias in my research because of the people who have been most helpful in responding may also be people that have a genuine interest, and passion for craft.

Discussion

The research was started by obtaining various books and articles pertaining to craft history, local craft, and craft in education. This aspect of the study was difficult due to lack of resources such as books and previous research on local craft and craft in education. Research had to be collected from outside of the United States for most of the craft education resources. Although these resources were helpful for providing information, it would have been more beneficial to be able to research United States craft education. Another issue found with research was the lack of books available at local college libraries. In the libraries of Nazareth College, and SUNY Fredonia, both of which offer craft classes, the amount of texts on craft was dismal. Shelves of books on art and art history are most prominent, while only a small section is dedicated to the crafts.

Next, to understand where to start in this research process, I determined which schools offer what type of classes in their art department. This was done by either researching course offerings on school websites or by calling school guidance counselors. When calling guidance counselors I often found that school staff needed to look up the art department, and read off course offerings to me. They did not know the course offerings offhand, and they were unaware which classes were craft classes as opposed to traditional art classes. Through this process, I have researched 54 public school districts in the region of Western New York. All of these schools had visual art department which included a Studio in Art course as well as other electives. From the research, all of these districts offered a Drawing and Painting elective, and a majority offer courses such as Sculpture, and or Graphic Design. Within these districts 10 of them had Contemporary Craft, or Studio in Craft course offerings. Twelve districts had classes labeled Creative Crafts, which I will discuss further. There were also many schools that did not offer Contemporary Craft or Studio in Craft courses, but had courses that are part of the craft field such as Ceramics, Textiles or Fiber Design, and Jewelry Design. School districts that had one or more of these classes numbered 32 out of the 54 school districts. Out of the school districts researched, six of them had absolutely no course offerings in the area of craft.

From my research findings, 19% of schools offered a Contemporary Craft or Studio in Craft course. I have also determined that more schools in the Rochester area offered craft courses than in the Buffalo area. When adding the numbers of Studio in Craft and Contemporary Craft courses along with such classes as Ceramics, Textiles or Fiber Design and Jewelry Design, the percentage of craft field courses jumps to 78%. This is a large percentage of schools that are addressing the area of craft in some way, even if the scope is limited.

From the research found, I also must discuss the course offering Creative Crafts. Twenty-two percent of school districts researched offered this class. Looking back to my previous definition of craft, my perspective, and the literature review, a Creative Crafts course may not always be considered as part of "Craft" course offerings. I don't feel that it represents an authentic version of craft knowledge, and may do more harm to the field than good. This course was often an overview of many areas of visual art including weaving, printmaking, painting, beading, and others. In some cases, this course does not even fulfill the art requirement for graduation. It was discovered that this course offers craft knowledge such as weaving, then the next lesson may be painting a face on a pumpkin. In my opinion this course could marginalize the field of craft, and more thorough research and investigation would need to be done before including this course in the bulk of my research.

Once it was determined which schools offer craft, I was able to research the actual curriculum of some of these programs. This was done by going online and finding curriculum maps off of school websites, and by calling and emailing craft teachers themselves to obtain these documents. For the most part these documents were easy to obtain, but in one case a district was reluctant to give out information because it was recently updated and had not been approved completely yet. Within the 19% of school districts that offer Contemporary Craft or Studio in Craft course offerings, I am focusing on curriculum of three public school districts in the Western New York area. I have obtained curriculum maps from each of these districts in order to review the content of these course offerings. When viewing these curriculum maps I looked for references to the Arts and Crafts Movement in the United States, local craft resources, local craft history, and local craft artisans, both historical and contemporary. I understand that a curriculum map cannot thoroughly explain the details of course content, yet it provides a valid starting point for understanding. These curriculum maps provided insight for this study yet left room for interpretation and questioning.

For example, in one district outside of Buffalo, their Studio in Craft curriculum map lays out the curriculum for units in ceramics and in jewelry design. This curriculum map shows that students will learn about the ancient history of craft such as Greek, Roman, Egyptian, and Renaissance craft and craftsmen, as well as study more contemporary craft artists. The craft artists mentioned in this curriculum map are Michael Lucero, New York City based ceramicist; Emily Schroeder, a Chicago based ceramicist; and Clare Graham, a Los Angeles based metals designer. There is no specific mentioning of the Arts and Crafts Movement, Western New York craft history, Western New York craft resources, or Western New York craft artists, both past and present.

In addition to Buffalo, a Rochester suburban school district's curriculum map for its Contemporary Craft course was included in the research. This map lays out the curriculum for units in fiber, jewelry and metals, alternative materials and paper arts. This curriculum map showed that students would gain an understanding of craft philosophy, and craftsmanship. Along with this the students will discuss ancient and contemporary craft history. The curriculum map outlines the importance of students researching contemporary craft artists, yet does not mention any artists in particular. Like the previous curriculum map, this map does not include any direct references to the Arts and Crafts Movement, Western New York craft history, Western New York craft resources, or Western New York craft artists, both past and present.

The final curriculum map investigated was slightly different from that of previous districts. This school district is in proximity to the Roycroft campus, and their studio in craft course is called The Roycroft Arts. Due to their direct proximity to the Roycroft campus, this curriculum map explored local craft more explicitly. This map shows the curriculum for mediums such as stained glass, block printing, ceramics, copper work, wood working and book making. The caveat listed explains that students will not create artworks in all mediums, but the class will explore many. This curriculum map also outlines to students the importance and the history of the Arts and Crafts movement. Students will learn about the important players of the Arts and Crafts movement, both locally and internationally. The students will also gain knowledge of important artworks within craft history based on information from this curriculum map. When discussing the region of Western New York, the curriculum map states, "[Students will] be able to explain what was the Roycroft Community's affect and contribution to the past and present East Aurora community." The curriculum does not specifically list any artists or any other craft resources other than the Roycroft in their curriculum map.

Even though I viewed three different curriculum maps, a full understanding of craft education in Western New York was not clear. I needed to understand teacher's opinion of craft, and what, and how they actually teach it. In order to more fully comprehend these craft courses, and their curriculum, I have spoken with the teachers who teach these classes, and one teacher in a district where craft is not offered as a course option. Due to time constraints, and many teacher's busy schedules, this was done through email interviewing. By using email, there may have been less stress, since the responses to my questions were quick and concise. This was also a detriment to my research because some of the answers I received were too concise, and I would have preferred more elaboration. By using the responses to my interviews, this helped in establishing whether local craft is prominent in teacher's living curriculum, even if it is not written in a curriculum map.

While discussing craft curriculum with teachers from the three districts, I have obtained a better understanding of what drives craft curriculum and classes. Teachers A and B are from suburban, public, school districts of mainly middle socioeconomic class, and their schools offer craft classes. Teacher C is from a public school district of a lower socioeconomic class, which did not offer craft classes. The teachers I interviewed were female art teachers that have been teaching an average of 22 years. Throughout their career these teachers expressed that they have seen many changes within the art education field. All the teachers are passionate about visual art, and felt that the crafts are in integral part of visual art. Teacher B explained that, "The craft classes offer a student a unique approach to the arts with a different approach than fine art." Teacher C advocates for craft by stating, "For some of our students their only success and worth [is in the crafts] and taking that opportunity away from our students is morally and educationally wrong."

Each of these teachers use local craft resources during their own personal time, such as the Rochester Memorial Art Gallery and the Burchfield Penney museum. They felt that it was important to use artists and cultures within their lessons to exemplify works of art. As Teacher A stated, "Yes, I include artist's work, ALWAYS." With that being said, even though these teachers visit local resources, and always include art history and culture within their lessons, only one out of the three used local artists within their lessons.

Teacher A explained that she uses local craft artists within her lessons. Students in this teacher's class do artist presentations to the class through a Microsoft PowerPoint presentation. These students are encouraged to explore local artists for this assignment. For other units in craft such as furniture, books, and ceramics, this teacher utilizes the artwork of Amie Freling Brown, Elizabeth Lyons, Nancy Jurs, Adam Spector, Peter Pincus, Bill Stewart and Stephen Merrit. These local artists are discussed, yet the extent to which they are used, and their influence on students cannot be determined in the scope of this study.

Although teachers are trying to create authentic craft experiences, one issue brought up by the teachers is budget. Budgets effect department size, course offerings, and curriculum. The departments at each of the schools have had different experiences. The department of teacher A has remained about the same size. Teacher B's department has expanded by one full-time position, and Teacher C's department has been reduced significantly. The size of the department has a direct influence on what courses can be taught. This means classes like Studio in Art, Drawing and Painting, and even AP Art may take precedence over a crafts class.

In addition to department size, budgets also affect the type, quantity and quality of supplies an art department can acquire. Every teacher expressed that they needed to be careful, and diligent with their materials and budget. Craft materials such as jewelry tools, metal, clay, and kilns have a high cost compared to colored pencils and paper, therefore a higher proportion of a departments who offer craft's budget may have to go towards craft supplies. Teacher B mentioned that her curriculum for the crafts class was often determined by the supply budget for that year. For example, due to the high cost of metal and jewelry supplies, that unit may be taken out of the course and another craft concept may be taught.

In continuing with budget problems, was the lack of outside of school opportunities afforded to students. The school districts for teachers B and C do not have any funding for field trips in their art departments. Even though this region has great craft resources, students cannot see them due to a lack of money or a fair appropriation of those funds within a school. In contrast, Teacher A's district was able to take many field trips with their craft classes. Some of these include More Fire Glass Studio, the Albert Paley studio, and students have seen a raku firing at Nazareth College. These field trip experiences motivated students, and gave them a better understanding of the craft field.

One district that showed a difference in the craft experience is the district in close proximity to the Roycroft campus. Their proximity to this resource makes their craft program very different from others. After trying to contact the craft teacher multiple times, but to no avail, I discovered an interview done by the Roycroft Campus Corporation with Ron VanOstrand, a craft teacher from that district. This interview helped to answer some questions as to why this district was so different from other districts when it come to their crafts course. Van Ostrand graduated from the School for American Craftsman at RIT, and is a Roycroft artisan. His specialty is metalsmithing and jewelry, and he teaches the Roycroft Arts class at East Aurora High School. Being a craftsman himself allows students to fully understand the process of craft, from the conceptualization to selling a piece. Students can go to the Roycroft and see their teacher's work for sale. This class is much more focused on local Arts and Crafts contributions, and Van Ostrand makes sure his students understand the history around them. Knowledge of the history and philosophy of the Roycroft is an integral component to the crafts class. This class has also made connections to the Roycroft campus, and VanOstrand encourages students to explore on their own. The literature and interviews on this program seem to position this as an exemplar of how craft classes can make meaningful connections with the vast array of local craft resources we have.

In some cases schools do not have the funds, connections or information to make use of resources like that of the district in proximity to the Roycroft appears to do. In these cases I feel that the craft resources and institutions themselves could reach out to districts to make those connections. I reached out to the program director of The Roycroft Campus Corporation, Alan Nowicki, to better understand the Roycroft's stance on education. We met for a long, unstructured interview, where we discussed the past, present, and future of education at the Roycroft campus. To see the general questions asked during this interview see Appendix B. The Roycroft Campus Corporation feels very strongly about educating the community and students about the Roycroft and its illustrious past. Nowicki is a former art educator, so he has a unique perspective on the importance of craft in curriculum.

For the past 2 years, Nowicki has been the program director for the Roycroft with a focus on education. He utilizes the Roycroft campus to bring educators and students in, as well as reach out to school districts. He creates programs for the Roycroft campus in all areas of the arts including visual, music, and performing arts. He also incorporates other subject areas into the Roycroft experience by reaching out to History and ELA teachers. He does this to build knowledge and recognition of the Roycroft name, so that it becomes prominent to more people than just artists.

According to Nowicki, he sees the future of the Roycroft involving many more educational experiences for students, and even lifelong learners. He stated that the philosophy of the Roycroft, such as "the head, the heart, and the hand" which was discussed previously, is something that all types of students can gain meaning from. It is a philosophy of living that is sustainable and rewarding, which complements education in the arts. Nowicki indicated that he was in the process of reaching out to communities, school districts, administrators, and educators to bring the meaning and historical importance to the forefront of people's minds in the Western New York area. One issue that Nowicki is dealing with is funding. Local districts do not have the money for field trips so this limits the amount of people the Roycroft can reach. The Roycroft Campus Corporation are considering putting together educational kits about the Roycroft to send out to schools. Nowicki is also promoting the Roycroft by bringing a national craft conference to the campus in October 2012. With the help of Nowicki, more educators could bring the Roycroft, and the Arts and Crafts Movement into their curriculum.

Unfortunately, Nowicki did not feel that the resources of the Roycroft are being utilized by local educators in the best way possible. For example, a class specifically for educators was offered twice by the Roycroft. This class included history, bookbinding, and even writing as part of a workshop. For the class description see Appendix C. The first time the class was ran no teachers signed up to attend. Not wanting to give up, the Roycroft ran the class again, and a total of 3 educators signed up for the class. This was disheartening for Nowicki and the Campus Corporation, and the Roycroft ceased to offer additional classes.

Analysis

Analyzing the data through a postmodern lens allowed myself to understand how craft is often treated differently than fine art, and how it is represented in education and the community. I have interpreted my data and interviews through this lens, and my own personal definition of craft, which has allowed me to make sense of my findings.

Considering this small study, it is evident craft's presence in the world of art is on a much smaller scale than fine art, solely based on literature. The amount of literature on fine art seems vastly superior to that of craft. Through my investigation some local colleges do not even have the texts to sufficiently explain and document craft history and contemporary craft artists. Therefore, when researching craft education I had to look extremely in-depth to find any information regarding this topic, and the information located was not from the United States. This seems to show that craft is still occupying a lower status than fine arts in the area of literature and research.

In relation to this, the number of craft classes within local art departments included in this study was a small minority. Since many other classes seemed to take precedence over craft classes. Studio in Art and Drawing and Painting are classes that are available in the vast majority of districts. Many districts are currently facing cuts in their departments, specifically the arts, so administration and educators must make decisions on which classes to keep. In my opinion, because the fine arts are held in greater esteem than the crafts, fine arts classes are kept in course offerings over craft classes. This was evidenced in Teacher C's district where jewelry and ceramics classes were offered, and now jewelry is no longer available, and ceramics is greatly reduced.

This reduction possibly connects to budgeting, which was also a major factor on craft in education. Craft classes require materials and tools that can be more expensive than typical art classes. This may lead to educators and administrators may be shying away from craft classes due to their monetary concerns. This may also lead to creating craft classes such as Creative Crafts, which may not be an authentic representation of craft based on my previous definition. Creative Crafts courses sometimes do not use traditional craft materials. Instead, based on research, these classes may use recycled objects which helps to keep costs down, yet could lead to a course that marginalizes the crafts.

When analyzing curriculum maps it becomes clear that all crafts courses are not created equal in relation to their focus on the Western New York region. In my opinion, the district closest to the Roycroft campus includes the most information about the history and culture of craft of Western New York in their curriculum map. With that being said, their curriculum may show bias based on their extreme proximity to a prominent, local craft resource. The other curriculum maps do not explicitly mention any Western New York craft resources or artists. This may indicate that using local resources is not foremost in most educators and curriculum writers minds.

When reviewing the interviews, I feel that there was a disconnect between what teachers said is important, and what was actually being taught in the classroom. All the teachers interviewed explained that they themselves feel strongly about craft, and utilize local resources. This is not shown in their curriculum or in their answers to the interviews. It was confusing why this is happening, but this may be due to classes having to always been taught in a certain way which did not include local resources. Another reason could be that teachers did not have a strong background in craft, and even if they felt passionate about it, they do not feel confident in teaching it.

After analyzing the situation of the Roycroft, it seemed that this prominent local craft resource was not being utilized properly. This was evidenced by the fact that local school districts do not often visit for field trips, although that could be due to budget issues. I also feel that this is evidenced by the fact that the Roycroft was trying to reach out to educators and offer classes, and the response they have received from local school teachers has been slim to none. If this is happening at a resource such as the Roycroft, than it may also be happening at other rich, local craft resources.

Conclusion

It is difficult to come to a definitive conclusion on craft in Western New York based on my limitations such as time, sample size and available participants. It is important to note the information I have found locally may not be generalizable across a wider group. There may be locations outside of Western New York that are experiencing something quite different from our region. Therefore, in conclusion, I feel that the history and culture of craft in Western New York is not reflected in the craft curriculum of some Western New York districts. Considering my findings, it is included in some ways, but not in an authentic and detailed way. This is unfortunate due to the vast number of craft resources that Western New York has, and it would be beneficial to understand the cause.

To obtain a clearer perspective on this particular issue, more in-depth research would need to be done. I would suggest a larger sample, and a more detailed and rigorous interviewing process. I would also suggest more research and discussion with local craft resources to determine how they intend to strengthen the connection between craft and art educators.

One interesting conclusion I have drawn from my research was that the disconnect between teacher's feelings about craft, and what they teach in their classrooms, may be due to their own background experience. Teachers who have not had adequate experience in the crafts themselves may not be presenting craft in their classroom in an authentic way. To understand this further it would be beneficial to survey and interview pre-service art educators on their experience, knowledge and comfortability with craft. It would also be of interest to see how these pre-service teachers write and teach a crafts-based lesson. This would help to determine how craft could genuinely be presented in the classroom.

Considering art education college programs, and pre-service art teachers, it is important to mention one interesting fact that was not included in the bulk of my research, and may bring more insight into craft at the college level. Metalsmith and professor Metcalf (1997) explained a personal anecdote about his own students. He indicated that most students have never taken a craft class before undergraduate school. Once in college some students may take one craft class, but the majority may never take another craft class, or rarely think about craft again. In his opinion however, a small number of students may decide to take another craft class, and if this happens, he believes that these students decide to major in the crafts. This anecdote has relevance because this has been my own experience, and possibly the experience of others. In reaction to this, it seems beneficial to find out just why this happens, and study the experiences of college students in the crafts.

Overall, the information gained in this study has helped to shed light on an issue in the Western New York region. The craft experience in Western New York is one that hopefully will continue to expand, and engage students in authentic crafts experience. Although it is unfortunate that Western New York craft resources seem to not be utilized effectively, it is important to note this as a possible opportunity for growth and more research. With continuing research more students may have the opportunity be exposed to the benefits of craft, and develop a lifelong interest in craft like I have experienced.

References

American Craft Council Awards (1997). *American Craft,* 57(5), 84.

American Crafts - RIT: College of Imaging Arts & Sciences. (n.d.). *RIT: College of Imaging Arts & Sciences*. Retrieved February 28, 2012, from http://cias.rit.edu/schools/american-crafts.

APA Manual (Publication manual of the American Psychological Association) (6th ed.). (2010). Washington, DC: American Psychological Association.

Boris, E. (1986). *Art and labor: Ruskin, Morris, and the craftsman ideal in America*. Philadelphia: Temple University Press.

Burnaford, G., Fischer, J., & Hobson, D. (Eds.). (2001) Teachers doing research: The power of action through inquiry (2nd ed.). Mahwah, NJ: Lawrence Erlbaum Associates.

Centennial Sculpture Park: Phase 1. (n.d.). *The Memorial Art Gallery*. Retrieved March 9, 2012, from mag.rochester.edu/centennial-sculpture-park/phase-1/.

Clancy, J. (2009). Elbert Hubbard, transcendentalism and the arts and crafts movement in America. *The Journal of Modern Craft, 2*(2), 143-160.

Cummings, W. K. (1999). The institutionS of education: Compare, compare, compare! *Comparative Education Review*, *43*(4), 413.

Cunningham, J. (2008). Conversations in western New York; Charles Rohlfs, and Gustav Stickley. *The Magazine Antiques, 173*(5), 120-129.

Dormer, P. (1997). *The culture of craft: status and future*. Manchester, UK: Manchester University Press.

Eisner, E. W. (1979). The use of qualitative forms of evaluation for improving educational practice. *American Educational Research Association*, *1*(6), 11-19.

Fariello, A. (2005). Albert Paley. *Metalsmith*, *25*(2), 42-49.

Fetterman, D. M., Qualitative approaches to evaluating education. *Educational Researcher, 17* (8), 17-23.

Greenhalgh, P. (2002). *The persistence of craft*. London: A. & C. Black.

Kangas, M. (2006). *Craft and concept: the re-materialization of the art object*. New York: Midmarch Arts Press.

Karppinen, S. (2008). Craft-art as a basis for human activity. *International Journal Of Art & Design Education, 27*(1), 83-90.

Kirwin, L. & Lord, J. (2003). A toolkit of dreams: Conversations with American craft artists. *Archives of American Art Journal, 43*(1/2), 1-24.

Koch, R. (1967). Elbert Hubbard's Roycrofters as artist-craftsmen. *Winterthur Portfolio, 3*, 67-82.

Koplos, J., & Metcalf, B. (2010). *Makers: a history of American studio craft*. Chapel Hill: University of North Carolina Press.

Ludwig, C. L. (1983). *The arts & crafts movement in New York State, 1890s-1920s*. Hamilton, N.Y.: Gallery Association of New York State.

Marshall, M. N. (1996) Sampling for qualitative research. *Family Practice, 13*(6), 522-525.

Mason, R. (2005). The meaning and value of home-based craft. *International Journal Of Art & Design Education, 24*(3), 261-268.

Metcalf, B. (2010). Craft's new borderland. *Metalsmith, 30*(1), 36-43.

Myers, M. D., & Newman, M. (2007) The qualitative interview in IS research: Examining the craft. *Information and Organization, 17*, 2–26.

Olafsson, B., & Thorsteinsson, G. (2009). Design and craft education in Iceland, pedagogical background and development: A literature review. *Design and Technology Education, 14* (2), 10-24.

Pollanen, S. (2009). Contextualising craft: Pedagogical models for craft education. *International Journal Of Art & Design Education, 28*(3), 249-260.

Rust, R., & Turgeon, K. (1999). *The Roycroft Campus*. Charleston: Arcadia Pub.

Short, E. C. (1987). *Curriculum Research in Retrospect.*

Simpson, T. (1994) Hand and home: The homes of American craftsmen. *American Craft, 57*(5), 46-53.

Smith, P. J., & Lucie-Smith, E. (1986). *Craft today: poetry of the physical*. New York: American Craft Museum.

Winchell, A. (2010). *Regretsy: where DIY meets WTF*. New York: Villard Books.

Zeeman, L., Poggenpoel, M., Myburgh, C., & Van Der Linde, N. (2002). An introduction to a postmodern approach to educational research: Discourse analysis. *Education, 123*(1), 96.

Appendices

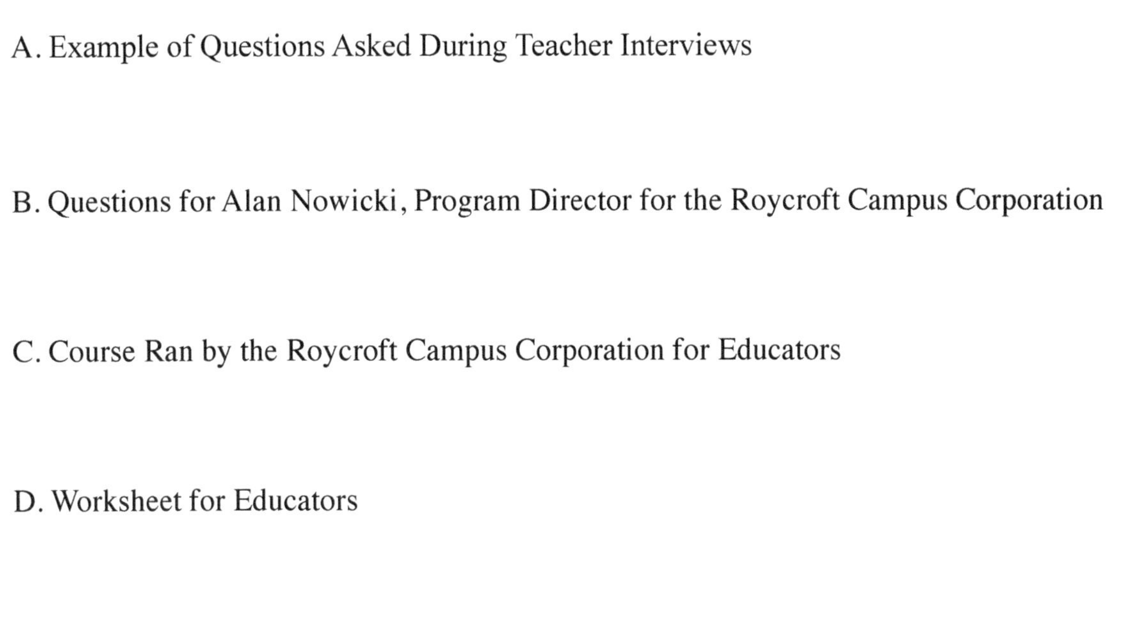

A. Example of Questions Asked During Teacher Interviews

B. Questions for Alan Nowicki, Program Director for the Roycroft Campus Corporation

C. Course Ran by the Roycroft Campus Corporation for Educators

D. Worksheet for Educators

E. Thesis Poster

Appendix A

Example of Questions Asked During Teacher Interviews

Questions

1. How long have you been teaching in the same district?

2. Has your department expanded or contracted since you've started?

3. Is there a contemporary craft class or studio in craft class at the high school level at your school?

4. Are there other craft classes at the high school level? (for example ceramics, fibers, jewelry, wood)

5. Has the area of craft expanded or contracted since you have been here?

6. If contracted or expanded, why do you think that is?

7. Is budget an issue with developing craft classes?

8. If a craft course is taught, do you include artist's work as examples for your students?

9. If yes to previous question, do you include artists from the Western New York Region? (if yes name them)

10. Do you discuss the Arts and Crafts movement in the Western New York area? Both historical and contemporary?

11. Has your crafts class gone on any field trips to explore craft in this region?

12. Have you yourself explored craft resources in this region? (RIT, Roycroft, Burchfield Penney, Paley Studios, etc)

13. Why or why not do you feel teaching craft is an important part of your department and course offerings?

14. Anything else you may want me to understand?

Appendix B

Questions for Alan Nowicki, Program Director for the Roycroft Campus Corporation

Questions

1. Why should local art teachers include the Roycroft and its history into their curriculum?

2. How does learning about the arts and crafts movement benefit students?

3. What does the Roycroft offer educators on campus?

4. Do educators come to the Roycroft?

5. Do schools take field trips to the Roycroft? Are they art or history classes? Other?

6. If schools can't take field trips, what are their options?

7. Do you send anyone out to schools?

8. What are the future plans for education at the Roycroft campus?

9. Do you think Roycroft artisans would consider doing an "artist in residence experience" in schools for students (like Young Audiences)?

10. Does the Roycroft influence contemporary craft?

11. Would the Roycroft consider being part of an informational packet geared towards art teachers that explained and promoted local craft resources?

Appendix C

Course Ran by the Roycroft Campus Corporation for Educators

Book Arts

Integrating Book Arts in the Classroom

(with Roycroft Renaissance Master Artisan, Diane Bond)* Special Educators Course *

Saturday, October 1st from 10:00am - 2:30pm

This course was designed specifically with teachers in mind. Participants will create a variety of simple handmade books or paper folded structures that they can take back and use in their classroom with students. We will discuss possibilities for applications within various subject areas, i.e. how to make handmade books to teach writing, math, science, art, etc. All structures can be made with simple tools like scissors, rulers, folding tools (popsicle sticks), pencils and glue. Bring your imagination, ideas and any questions you may have. A lunch will be provided during the workshop. A certificate will be given upon completion of the course for possible district P.D. credit. (Please check with your individual district to make sure these hours will be accepted).

Diane Bond is a Roycroft Renaissance Master Artisan in book arts. She has been an Artisan since 2006 and achieved master status in 2010. She graduated from Buffalo State College with a bachelor's degree in both graphic design and art education and a master's degree in art education. She worked as a freelance graphic designer at Fisher-Price Toys, the Buffalo News and was an apprentice bookbinder for the Soleil Bookbindery in Rochester. Diane worked at Lancaster High School as an art educator for many years and currently teaches in the Orchard Park School District. She has taught courses at area colleges and numerous bookmaking workshops all across Western New York. She also serves on the Board of Directors for the Western New York Book Arts Center.

Diane has exhibited her work at the Burchfield-Penney Art Center, the Western New York Book Arts Center, the University of Buffalo, the Impact Gallery and the Roycroft Winter Show. Her work was included in ***500 Handmade Books***, published by Lark Books.

Class Tuition $60 members - $65 non-members + $10 Supplies =

$70* members - $75* non-members

Registration is required and seating is limited (Max. of 12 students)

* Fee includes a lunch

To register please call the Roycroft Copper Shop at **716-655-0261** or visit our website at www.roycroftcampuscorporation.com

Roycroft Copper Shop Gallery - 31 South Grove St. East Aurora, NY 14052

Appendix D

Worksheet for Educators

Know Your Local Craft Resources

Make sure to discuss our region's vast history in the Arts and Craft's movement. Key artists include, Dard Hunter, Karl Kipp, Adelaide Alsop Robineau, Gustav Stickley, Charles Rohlfs, and even Corning and Oneida are players in this movement.

HERE ARE A FEW OPTIONS

The Roycroft Campus Corporation
31 South Grove Street
East Aurora, NY 14052
716.655.0261

Burchfield Penney Art Center
1300 Elmwood Avenue
Buffalo, NY 14222
716.878.6011
burchfld@buffalostate.edu

More Fire Glass Studio
80 Rockwood Place
Rochester, New York 14610
585.242.0450
Email: info@morefireglass.com

Paley Studios, Ltd.
1677 Lyell Ave
Suite A
Rochester, NY 14606
585.232.5260
info@albertpaley.com

School for American Crafts
College of Imaging Arts and Sciences
73 Lomb Memorial Drive
Rochester, NY 14623-5603
585.475.6114
sac@rit.edu

Memorial Art Gallery of the University of Rochester
500 University Ave.
Rochester, NY 14607
585.276.8900

At The Roycroft Campus, East Aurora NY

At RIT School for American Craftsmen, Rochester NY

Elizabeth Lyons, Rochester NY

Many local craft artists are extremely approachable. Field trips to local sites, as well as artists in residence programs, and even skyping with local artists is a great opportunity for students.

By Megan Westenfield 2012

Appendix D

Thesis Poster

How is the History and Culture of Craft in Western New York Reflected in the Contemporary Craft Curriculum of Selected Western New York Districts?

Rationale

- My personal interest in craft throughout my childhood and college experience has led me to be a passionate supporter of craft in art education.

-The local area of Western New York has a wide variety of craft resources, (as evidenced by this NYS map) and can be described as the incubator for the U.S. Arts and Crafts Movement.

-It is unclear whether local teachers are utilizing their local craft resources for the benefit of the students in their classroom.

-There are currently no other studies of this issue in our region, and therefore this study intends to shed light on this topic.

Literature

-Much literature has been written on the history of craft, and craft artisans themselves. Much less has been written on craft in education.

-Nordic countries such as Finland believe craft education, or Sloyd education, is an integral part of a well-rounded student.

-In the U.S. most students will not experience a craft course until college, and will not experience craft again.

-Craft allows the brain a to exercise the bodily kinesthetic intelligence as evidenced by research from Howard Gardner.

-Craft in New York State, specifically Western New York, has a prominent well-known history and this region is also home to a variety of celebrated contemporary craftsmen.

Methods

-This study is qualitative in nature, and utilizes mixed methods for obtaining data.

-Research on which local schools have craft course was done first.

-A curriculum review of craft curriculum maps was done using data from three different school districts across Western New York. This was done using the method of comparative inquiry.

-Next, three art teachers were interviewed about their feelings on craft, and local craft resources. These were structured interviews.

-Also, interviews were done of a noted craft historian, and the program director for The Roycroft Campus. These were more informal, unstructured interviews.

Participants

-Participants in this study were most school districts in the Buffalo and Rochester areas.

-Curriculum maps from three districts that teach craft were part of my sample.

-Three art teachers from various districts, two with craft classes and one without were interviewed.

-Author Robert Rust was interviewed for more in-depth information regarding the Arts and Crafts Movement, specifically in Western New York.

-Program director for The Roycroft Campus Corporation Alan Nowicki was interviewed to gain a better understanding of how craft resources reach out to districts.

Findings

-There is a disconnect between what teachers feel is important, and what they are teaching in their classes.

-Teachers utilize local craft resources themselves, yet commonly fail to integrate them into their craft curriculum.

-Issues like budgets have a major influence on the quality and type of craft classes offered.

-Local craft resources such as the Roycroft try to reach out to educators, but often do not see a strong response.

Implications

-Due to the nature and limitations of this study, my findings are not generalizable across the craft field.

-More research must be done as to why teachers are not utilizing local craft resources in a meaningful and authentic way.

-Research into pre-service teacher education, and their craft experience, may be beneficial to develop a better understanding of why local craft resources are not integrated properly.

References

Boris, E. (1986). Art and labor: Ruskin, Morris, and the craftsman ideal in America. Philadelphia: Temple University Press.

Dormer, P. (1997). The culture of craft: status and future. Manchester, UK: Manchester University Press.

Greenhalgh, P. (2002). The persistence of craft. London: A. & C. Black.

Kangas, M. (2006). Craft and concept: the re-materialization of the art object. New York: Midmarch Arts Press.

Karppinen, S. (2008). Craft-art as a basis for human activity. International Journal Of Art & Design Education, 27(1), 83-90.

Koplos, J., & Metcalf, B. (2010). Makers: a history of American studio craft. Chapel Hill: University of North Carolina Press.

Ludwig, C. L. (1983). The arts & crafts movement in New York State, 1890s-1920s. Hamilton, N.Y.: Gallery Association of New York State.

Mason, R. (2005). The meaning and value of home-based craft. International Journal Of Art & Design Education, 24(3), 261-268.

Metcalf, B. (2010). Craft's new borderland. Metalsmith, 30(1), 36-43.

Olafsson, B., & Thorsteinsson, G. (2009). Design and craft education in Iceland, pedagogical background and development: A literature review. Design and Technology Education, 14(2), 10-24.

Pollanen, S. (2009). Contextualising craft: Pedagogical models for craft education. International Journal Of Art & Design Education, 28(3), 249-260.

Rust, R., & Turgeon, K. (1999). The Roycroft Campus. Charleston: Arcadia Pub.

Smith, P. J., & Lucie-Smith, E. (1986). Craft today: poetry of the physical. New York: American Craft Museum.

Winchell, A. (2010). Regretsy: where DIY meets WTF. New York: Villard Books.

By Megan Westenfield
Nazareth College

www.ingramcontent.com/pod-product-compliance
Ingram Content Group UK Ltd.
Pitfield, Milton Keynes, MK11 3LW, UK
UKHW051135260726
13967UKWH00010B/3067